EMBRACING YOUR UNIQUENESS

SECRET STRATEGIES FOR LIVING AN AUTHENTIC LIFE

DR. JAGADEESH PILLAI

Made with ♥ on the Notion Press Platform
www.notionpress.com

|| Dedicated to all wisdom seekers around the world ||

❦❦❦

Contents

Contents

Prayer

"Om Bhadram Karnebhih Shrunuyaama DevaahBhadram Pashyemaakshabhiryajatraah Sthirairangaistushtuvaamsastanoobhih Vyashema Devahitam YadaayuhSwasti Na Indro VridhashravaahSwasti Nah Pooshaa VishwavedaahSwasti Nastaarkshyo ArishtanemihSwasti No Brihaspatir DadhaatuOm Shantih, Shantih, Shantih"

The literal meaning of this mantra is: OM. O Gods! Let us hear auspicious words from our ears. O reverent Gods! Let us behold propitious visions from our eyes, let our organs and body be stable, healthy, and strong. Let us do that which is pleasing to the gods in the life span allotted to us. May Indra, inscribed in the scriptures, bring us fortune! May Pushan, the knower of the world, grant us prosperity! May Trakshya, who vanquishes enemies, bestow us with blessings! May Brihaspati bring us success!
OM Peace, Peace, Peace.

About The Author

Dr. Jagadeesh Pillai is a renowned Guinness World Record holder, writer, and researcher hailing from Varanasi, also known as the abode of Lord Shiva. With a Ph.D. in Vedic Science and a range of creative ideas and achievements, he is a true polymath. He is the author of more than 100 books including Research Publications. Although his roots can be traced back to Kerala, the people of Varanasi hold him in high regard and affectionately consider him one of their own.

In 1998, Dr. Pillai was offered a job at Banaras Hindu University, but he left the position after only two months to pursue greater goals in life. He believed that in order to study Indian scriptures and engage in other creative endeavours, he needed to retire from the daily grind of working solely for money at a young age.

He started an export business from scratch, using the knowledge he had gained from a previous job in the industry. His intelligence and unique approach to business led to great success in a short period of time, earning him more in just a decade and a half than he would have in a lifetime working in a government job. Upon the passing of Dr. APJ Abdul Kalam, Dr. Pillai decided to leave the business and dedicate himself to reading, studying, researching, and experimenting.

During his tenure in the export business, Dr. Pillai traveled to over 16 countries, gaining valuable insight and experiencing the world and life in detail.

Dr. Pillai has achieved four Guinness World Records in the following subjects:

"Script to Screen" - In this record, Dr. Pillai produced and directed an animation film within the shortest time possible, breaking the previous record set by Canadians. He has also received numerous national and international awards and recognitions for this achievement.

Longest Line of Postcards - For this record, Dr. Pillai created a line of 16,300 postcards on the occasion of the 163rd anniversary of Indian Postal Day. The event also included a questionnaire about the Indian flag.

Largest Poster Awareness Campaign - Dr. Pillai designed an awareness campaign on the subject of "Beti Bachao - Beti Padhao" (Save the Girl Child - Educate the Girl Child) to achieve this record.

Largest Envelope - In tribute to the Indian Prime Minister's "Make in India" initiative, Dr. Pillai created a 4000 square meter envelope using waste paper to achieve this record.

Attempted - **70000 Candles on a 210 kg Cake** - To celebrate the 70th Indian Independence Day, Dr. Pillai attempted to light 70,000 candles on a 210 kg cake, which was recorded in World Records India.

Attempted - **Documentary on Dhamek Stupa of Sarnath in 17 Languages** - Dr. Pillai attempted to create a documentary on the Dhamek Stupa of Sarnath, dubbing it in 17 different languages. The result of this attempt is currently awaiting confirmation from the Guinness World Records.

Dr. Pillai is skilled in teaching the Bhagavad Gita, a Hindu scripture, and is popular among young people. He has helped many young people improve their lives through his motivational teachings.

In addition to teaching, he has composed and sung numerous Sanskrit Bhajans and patriotic songs.

He has also written and directed several short films and documentaries for awareness campaigns, and has volunteered with the police in both UP and Kerala to spread awareness about various issues through videos and photography.

Incredibly, he has produced and directed over 100 documentaries about the city of Varanasi, all on his own.

He has also helped and guided more than 25 boys and girls to achieve world records through creative and innovative methods. He is a multifaceted person who uses his intellect and the blessings given to him by God to excel in various areas. He is both a teacher and a student, always learning and teaching, and is able to master any subject he comes across.

He is a selfless social activist and motivational speaker who has overcome struggles and failures to become a successful and enthusiastic individual with a rich life experience.

In addition to his work with the Bhagavad Gita, he is also an efficient Tarot card reader, Astro-Vastu consultant, and a talented singer and composer. He has sung the entire Ram Charita Manas and Bhagavad Gita in his own compositions, and has sung the phrase "Lokah Samastha Sukhino Bhavantu" in 50 different languages. He is currently working on a detailed and scientific study of Vedas, Upanishads, Puranas, and the Bhagavad Gita. He has also composed and sung the Hanuman Chalisa and Gayatri Mantra in 108 and 1008 different compositions, respectively.

Awards - Four Times Guinness World Records, Winner of Mahatma Gandhi Vishwa Shanti Puraskar, Mahatma Gandhi Global Peace Ambassador, Kashi Ratna Award, Dr. APJ Abdul Kalam Motivational Person of the Year 2017, Mother Teresa Award, Indira Gandhi Priyadarshini Award, Bharat Vikas Ratna Award, Udyog Ratna Award, Vigyan Prasar Award, Poorvanchal Ratn Samman.

Preface

We all have a unique story to tell, and in Embracing Your Uniqueness: Secret Strategies for Living an Authentic Life, we explore the power of embracing our individual stories and how to use them to live a more fulfilling life. Through this book, we will uncover the secrets to living an authentic life and how to use our unique experiences to create a life of purpose and joy.

This book is a journey of self-discovery and exploration. It is a guide to understanding our individual stories and how to use them to create a life of meaning and purpose. We will explore the power of embracing our uniqueness and how to use it to create a life of joy and fulfillment.

We will also discuss the importance of self-care and how to use it to create a life of balance and harmony. We will explore the power of self-love and how to use it to create a life of abundance and joy. Finally, we will discuss the importance of living an authentic life and how to use it to create a life of purpose and fulfillment.

This book is a guide to understanding our individual stories and how to use them to create a life of meaning and purpose. Through this book, we will uncover the secrets to living an authentic life and how to use our unique experiences to create a life of joy and fulfillment. We will explore the power of embracing our uniqueness and how to use it to create a life of abundance and joy. We will also discuss the importance of self-care and how to use it to create a balance and harmony in our lives. Finally, we will discuss the importance of living an authentic life and how to use it to create a life of purpose and fulfillment.

This book is an invitation to explore the power of embracing our uniqueness and how to use it to create a life of joy and fulfillment. It is a journey of self-discovery and exploration, and a guide to understanding our individual stories and how to use them

As we navigate through life, it can be easy to forget that we are all unique individuals with our own unique stories to tell. In "Embracing Your Uniqueness: Secret Strategies for Living an Authentic Life," readers will discover the power of embracing their individual strengths and weaknesses, and learn how to use them to create a life of purpose and fulfillment.

This book is a guide to help readers uncover their true selves and live an authentic life. It provides practical strategies for recognizing and celebrating our unique qualities, and offers advice on how to use them to create meaningful connections with others. Through personal stories, exercises, and inspiring quotes, readers will gain insight into their own unique gifts and learn how to use them to create a life of purpose and joy.

This book is a must-read for anyone looking to live a life of authenticity and purpose. It is a powerful reminder that we are all unique and that our uniqueness is something to be celebrated. By embracing our individual strengths and weaknesses, we can create a life of meaning and fulfillment. So, if you're ready to take the journey to discover your true self and live an authentic life, then this book is for you.

ONE

UNDERSTANDING THE POWER OF UNIQUENESS

Uniqueness is a powerful force that can be used to create a life of authenticity and fulfillment. It is the key to unlocking our true potential and living a life that is true to ourselves.

At its core, uniqueness is about embracing our individual differences and celebrating them. It is about recognizing that we are all unique and that our differences should be celebrated, not judged. It is about understanding that our uniqueness is our strength and that it can be used to create a life of purpose and meaning.

Uniqueness is also about recognizing that we are all connected. We are all part of the same human family and our differences should be seen as a source of strength, not a source of division. We should strive to create a world where everyone is accepted and respected for who they are.

Uniqueness is also about understanding that our uniqueness is our power. It is the key to unlocking our true potential and living a life that is true to ourselves. It is about recognizing that our uniqueness is our strength and that it can be used to create a life of purpose and meaning.

Uniqueness is a powerful force that can be used to create a life of authenticity and fulfillment. It is the key to unlocking our true potential and living a life that is true to ourselves. By embracing our individual differences and celebrating them, we can create a world where everyone is accepted and respected for who they are. We can use our uniqueness to create a life of purpose and meaning, and to unlock our true potential. By understanding the power of uniqueness, we can live an authentic life and create a world of acceptance and understanding.

"The only limit to our realization of tomorrow will be our doubts of today."

TWO

BECOMING AWARE OF YOUR TRUE SELF

Becoming aware of your true self is an essential part of living an authentic life. It can be a difficult journey, but it is one that is ultimately rewarding. To begin, it is important to take a step back and reflect on who you are and what makes you unique.

Start by asking yourself questions such as: What are my core values? What are my passions? What do I believe in? What makes me different from others? What are my strengths and weaknesses?

As you answer these questions, you will begin to gain a better understanding of your true self. You may also find that you have been living in a way that is not in alignment with your true self. This can be a difficult realization, but it is an important step in the journey of self-discovery.

Once you have identified your true self, it is important to take action to live in alignment with it. This may involve making changes to your lifestyle, such as spending more time doing activities that bring you joy or surrounding yourself with people who share your values. It may also involve taking risks and pushing yourself out of your comfort zone.

Living an authentic life is not always easy, but it is worth the effort. When you are living in alignment with your true self, you will feel more fulfilled and content. You will also be more likely to attract positive experiences and relationships into your life.

By becoming aware of your true self and taking steps to live in alignment with it, you can unlock the power of your uniqueness and create a life that is truly authentic.

"You are never too old to set another goal or to dream a new dream."

THREE

Accepting Your Strengths and Weaknesses

Creating a daily routine for self-discipline is essential for achieving your goals. It can be difficult to stay motivated and focused on your goals, but having a daily routine can help you stay on track. Here are some tips for building a daily routine that will help you cultivate self-discipline:

1. **Start your day with a plan**. Before you begin your day, take a few moments to plan out what you want to accomplish. This will help you stay focused and motivated throughout the day.

2. **Set realistic goals**. It's important to set realistic goals that you can actually achieve. This will help you stay motivated and on track.

3. **Break down tasks into smaller chunks**. Breaking down

tasks into smaller chunks can make them more manageable and easier to complete.

4. Prioritize tasks. Prioritizing tasks can help you stay focused and organized.

5. Take breaks. Taking regular breaks throughout the day can help you stay focused and energized.

6. Reward yourself. Rewarding yourself for completing tasks can help you stay motivated and on track.

Creating a daily routine for self-discipline is an important step in achieving your goals. By following these tips, you can create a routine that will help you stay focused and motivated. With a daily routine in place, you can cultivate self-discipline and reach your goals.

"The only way to do great work is to love what you do."

FOUR

Overcoming Fear and Self-Doubt

Fear and self-doubt can be paralyzing, preventing us from living our most authentic lives. But with the right strategies, we can learn to overcome these obstacles and embrace our unique selves.

The first step in overcoming fear and self-doubt is to recognize that they are normal and natural. Everyone experiences fear and self-doubt at some point in their lives. It's important to remember that these feelings are not a sign of weakness, but rather a sign of strength. By acknowledging our fears and doubts, we can begin to take steps to address them.

The next step is to identify the source of our fear and self-doubt. Is it a fear of failure? A fear of rejection? A fear of the unknown? Once we have identified the source, we can begin to take action to address it.

One way to do this is to challenge our negative thoughts. When we find ourselves thinking negative thoughts, we can take a step back and ask ourselves if these thoughts are really true. We can also practice positive self-talk, reminding ourselves of our strengths and abilities.

Another way to overcome fear and self-doubt is to take small steps. Instead of trying to tackle our fears and doubts all at once, we can break them down into smaller, more manageable tasks. This can help us to feel more in control and less overwhelmed.

Finally, it's important to remember that we are not alone. We can reach out to friends, family, and professionals for support. Talking to someone who understands can help us to gain perspective and find the courage to move forward.

By recognizing our fears and doubts, challenging our negative thoughts, taking small steps, and seeking support, we can learn to overcome fear and self-doubt and embrace our unique selves. With the right strategies, we can live an authentic life and be true to who we are.

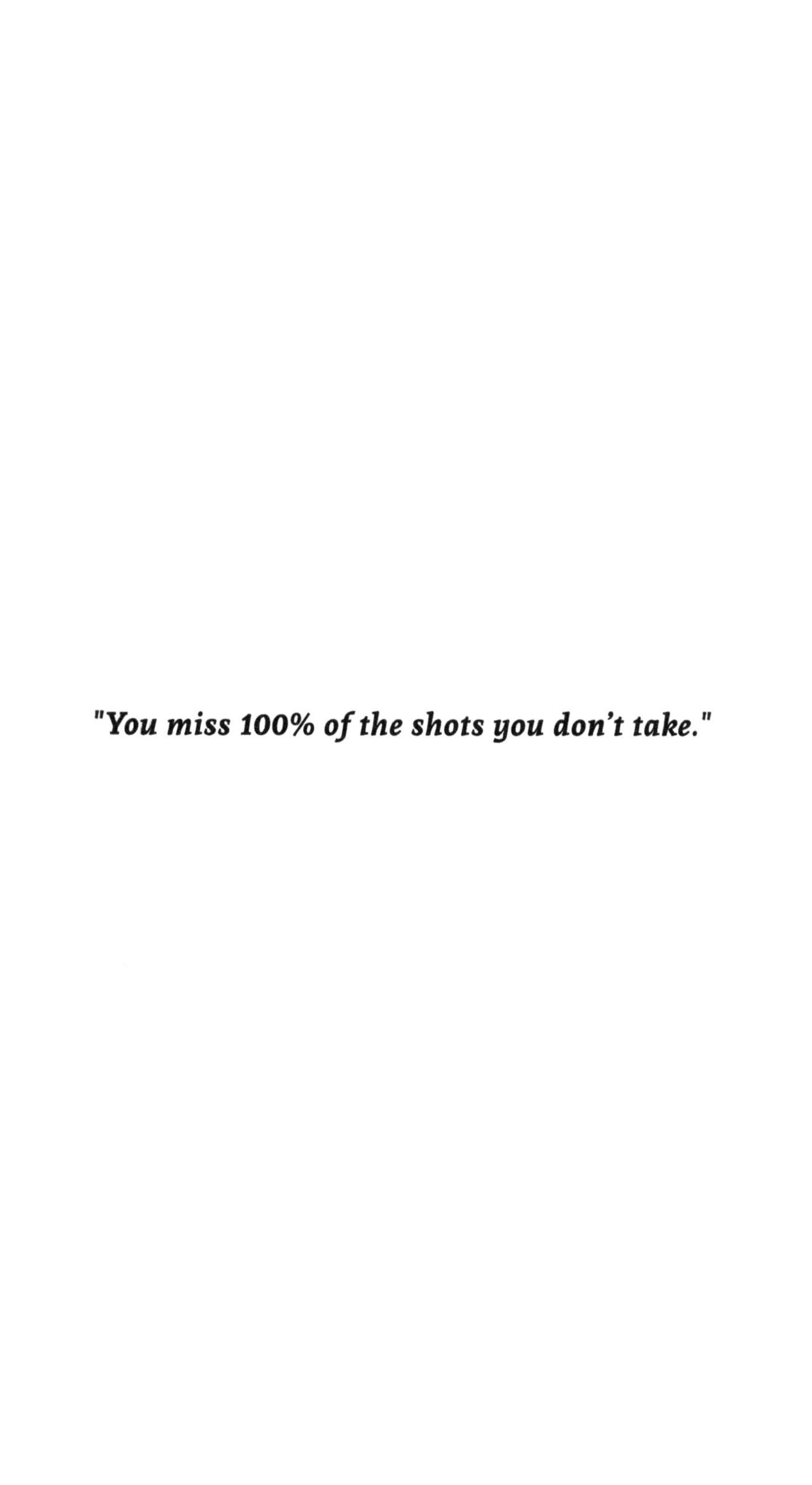

"You miss 100% of the shots you don't take."

FIVE

Developing Your Own Path

Everyone has their own unique journey in life, and it is important to recognize and embrace this. By understanding your own individual strengths and weaknesses, you can create a path that is tailored to your own needs and goals.

The first step in developing your own path is to identify your values and beliefs. What do you stand for? What do you believe in? What are your core values? Once you have identified these, you can begin to create a plan that is in line with your values and beliefs.

The next step is to set goals. What do you want to achieve? What do you want to accomplish? Setting goals will help you stay focused and motivated. It is important to set realistic goals that are achievable and measurable.

Once you have identified your values and set goals, it is time to take action. Taking action is the only way to make progress. It is important to take small steps and celebrate each success. This will help you stay motivated and on track.

Finally, it is important to stay flexible and open to change. Life is unpredictable and things don't always go as planned. It is important to be open to new opportunities and to adjust your plan as needed.

Developing your own path is an ongoing process. It requires dedication and hard work, but it is worth it. By embracing your uniqueness and creating a plan that is tailored to your individual needs and goals, you can live an authentic life and achieve your dreams.

"The greatest glory in living lies not in never falling, but in rising every time we fall."

SIX

LISTENING TO YOUR INNER VOICE

Listening to your inner voice is an essential part of living an authentic life. It is the voice of your intuition, your higher self, and your inner wisdom. It is the voice that speaks to you when you are in a quiet place, away from the noise and distractions of the world. It is the voice that guides you to make decisions that are in alignment with your true self.

Learning to listen to your inner voice can be a challenge, especially in a world that is filled with so much noise and distraction. It requires practice and patience. Start by taking time each day to be still and quiet. Find a comfortable place to sit and close your eyes. Take a few deep breaths and allow yourself to relax. As you sit in stillness, notice the thoughts and feelings that come up. Pay attention to the subtle messages that your inner voice is sending you.

Your inner voice is always speaking to you, but it can be difficult to hear it over the noise of the world. To strengthen your connection to your inner voice, practice mindfulness and meditation. Spend time in nature and observe the beauty and peace that surrounds you. Connect with your spiritual practice and ask for guidance.

When you listen to your inner voice, you will be able to make decisions that are in alignment with your true self. You will be able to trust your intuition and make choices that are right for you. You will be able to live an authentic life that is filled with joy and purpose.

Listening to your inner voice is an important part of embracing your uniqueness and living an authentic life. Take time each day to be still and quiet, and allow yourself to connect with your inner wisdom. As you practice listening to your inner voice, you will be able to make decisions that are in alignment with your true self and live a life that is filled with joy and purpose.

"Success is not final, failure is not fatal: it is the courage to continue that counts."

SEVEN

LEARNING TO TRUST YOURSELF

Learning to trust yourself is an essential part of living an authentic life. It can be difficult to trust yourself when you feel like you don't have the answers or don't know what to do. But with practice and dedication, you can learn to trust yourself and your decisions.

The first step to learning to trust yourself is to recognize that you have the power to make decisions. You may not always have the answers, but you can trust that you have the ability to make the best decision for yourself. It's important to remember that you are the only one who knows what is best for you.

The next step is to practice self-reflection. Take time to reflect on your decisions and how they have impacted your life. Ask yourself questions like, "What did I learn from this experience?" and "What could I have done differently?" This will help you gain insight into your decision-making process and build trust in yourself.

It's also important to practice self-compassion. When you make a mistake, don't beat yourself up. Instead, be kind to yourself and recognize that mistakes are part of the learning process. Acknowledge your mistakes, learn from them, and move on.

Finally, take risks. Taking risks can be scary, but it's also a great way to build trust in yourself. When you take risks, you're showing yourself that you can handle whatever comes your way. You may not always make the right decision, but you'll learn from it and become more confident in your ability to make decisions.

Learning to trust yourself is an important part of living an authentic life. It takes practice and dedication, but with time and effort, you can learn to trust yourself and your decisions. By recognizing your power to make decisions, practicing self-reflection, being kind to yourself, and taking risks, you can build trust in yourself and live an authentic life.

"The best way to predict your future is to create it."

EIGHT

EXPLORING YOUR PASSIONS AND INTERESTS

Exploring your passions and interests is an essential part of living an authentic life. It can be difficult to identify what truly drives you, but it is worth the effort. Taking the time to explore your passions and interests can help you discover your unique purpose and create a life that is meaningful and fulfilling.

Start by reflecting on what you enjoy doing. What activities bring you joy and satisfaction? What topics do you find yourself drawn to? What do you find yourself talking about with others? These are all clues to your passions and interests.

Once you have identified some of your passions and interests, it is time to explore them further. Take the time to research and learn more about the topics that interest you.

Read books, watch documentaries, and talk to people who are knowledgeable about the subject. This will help you gain a deeper understanding of your passions and interests.

You can also explore your passions and interests by trying new activities. Take a class, join a club, or volunteer for a cause that aligns with your interests. This will give you the opportunity to gain new skills and experiences.

Finally, take the time to reflect on what you have learned. How have your passions and interests shaped your life? What have you learned about yourself? How can you use your passions and interests to create a life that is meaningful and fulfilling?

Exploring your passions and interests is an important part of living an authentic life. It can help you discover your unique purpose and create a life that is full of joy and satisfaction. Take the time to reflect on what you enjoy doing, research topics that interest you, and try new activities. By doing so, you can gain a deeper understanding of yourself and use your passions and interests to create a life that is truly your own.

"The only true wisdom is in knowing you know nothing."

NINE

Managing Your Personal Responsibilities

Managing your personal responsibilities is an essential part of living an authentic life. It can be difficult to juggle all of the tasks and obligations that come with being an adult, but with the right strategies, you can learn to manage your responsibilities in a way that allows you to stay true to yourself.

The first step in managing your personal responsibilities is to prioritize. Make a list of all of your tasks and obligations, and then rank them in order of importance. This will help you to focus on the most important tasks first, and ensure that you don't get overwhelmed by the sheer number of things you need to do.

Next, create a schedule. This will help you to stay organized and ensure that you don't miss any important deadlines.

Make sure to include time for yourself in your schedule, as this will help you to stay balanced and avoid burnout.

Finally, don't be afraid to ask for help. Whether it's from family, friends, or colleagues, having a support system can make a huge difference when it comes to managing your responsibilities. Don't be afraid to reach out and ask for assistance when you need it.

By following these steps, you can learn to manage your personal responsibilities in a way that allows you to stay true to yourself. Prioritizing your tasks, creating a schedule, and asking for help when needed are all essential components of living an authentic life. With the right strategies, you can learn to manage your responsibilities and still have time to enjoy the things that make you unique.

"The secret of getting ahead is getting started."

TEN

Connecting With Your Community

Connecting with your community is an essential part of living an authentic life. It can be difficult to find your place in the world, but by connecting with your local community, you can create meaningful relationships and gain a sense of belonging.

One of the best ways to connect with your community is to get involved in local activities and events. Whether it's volunteering at a soup kitchen, attending a town hall meeting, or joining a local sports team, there are plenty of ways to get involved and make a difference. Not only will you be able to meet new people and make new friends, but you'll also be able to contribute to the betterment of your community.

Another great way to connect with your community is to

attend local festivals and celebrations. These events are a great way to learn about the culture and history of your area, as well as to meet new people and make new friends. Whether it's a music festival, a food festival, or a cultural celebration, attending these events can be a great way to get to know your community and make meaningful connections.

Finally, connecting with your community can also be done through online platforms. Social media is a great way to stay connected with your local community, as well as to find out about upcoming events and activities. You can also join online forums and discussion groups to connect with like-minded people and learn more about your local area.

Connecting with your community is an important part of living an authentic life. By getting involved in local activities, attending festivals and celebrations, and connecting with your community online, you can create meaningful relationships and gain a sense of belonging. So, take the time to explore your local area and get to know your community - you won't regret it!

"Believe in yourself and all that you are. Know that there is something inside you that is greater than any obstacle."

ELEVEN

Changing Habits to Live an Authentic Life

To live an authentic life, one must be willing to make changes to their habits and behaviors. It is not enough to simply think about making changes; one must take action and make the necessary adjustments.

The first step to living an authentic life is to identify the habits that are holding you back. These could be anything from unhealthy eating habits to negative thought patterns. Once you have identified the habits that are preventing you from living an authentic life, it is time to start making changes.

Start by making small changes. For example, if you are trying to break an unhealthy eating habit, start by replacing one unhealthy snack with a healthier option. This small change will help you to slowly break the habit and create a healthier lifestyle.

Another way to make changes is to create a plan. Set goals and create a timeline for yourself. This will help you stay on track and make sure that you are making progress.

Finally, it is important to remember that change takes time. It is not something that happens overnight. Be patient with yourself and don't give up.

Living an authentic life is not easy, but it is possible. By making small changes and creating a plan, you can start to break old habits and create new ones. With dedication and perseverance, you can live an authentic life that is true to who you are.

"The more you know yourself, the less you are prone to making ethical mistakes."

- J.C. Watts

♡♡♡

TWELVE

Creating a Supportive Environment

Creating a supportive environment is a crucial aspect of living an authentic life. A supportive environment provides the foundation for growth, self-discovery, and fulfillment. It enables individuals to feel safe, accepted, and valued, allowing them to express their unique qualities and pursue their passions and aspirations.

One of the key components of a supportive environment is the presence of positive and uplifting relationships. Surrounding oneself with individuals who encourage, support, and challenge us can provide the motivation and inspiration needed to pursue our goals and live our best lives.

It is also important to create a physical environment that supports our well-being and personal growth. This can involve decluttering, organizing, and creating a space that inspires creativity and positivity.

In addition, it is important to engage in activities and pursue interests that bring joy and fulfillment. This can involve pursuing hobbies, volunteering, or engaging in physical exercise. By engaging in activities that bring meaning and purpose, individuals can find a sense of satisfaction and fulfillment in life.

Lastly, it is important to seek out a community of like-minded individuals who share similar interests and values. This can involve joining a club, attending events, or participating in online communities. Having a sense of belonging and connection to others can provide a sense of support and encouragement, enabling individuals to embrace their uniqueness and live an authentic life.

In conclusion, creating a supportive environment is essential for living an authentic life. By surrounding oneself with positive relationships, creating a physical environment that supports well-being, engaging in fulfilling activities, and seeking out a community of like-minded individuals, individuals can cultivate the conditions necessary for personal growth, self-discovery, and fulfillment.

"Happiness is not something ready-made. It comes from your own actions."

- Dalai Lama

♡♡♡

THIRTEEN

Making Self-Care a Priority

Self-care is the practice of taking time to nurture and care for oneself, both physically and mentally. It is about recognizing our own needs and taking the necessary steps to meet them.

When we make self-care a priority, we are investing in our own wellbeing. We are taking the time to listen to our bodies and minds, and to respond to their needs. This can include anything from getting enough sleep, to eating healthy meals, to taking time for relaxation and reflection. It is about creating a balance between our physical, mental, and emotional needs.

Self-care is also about recognizing our own unique needs and taking the time to meet them. This could include anything from taking a yoga class to reading a book, to spending time with friends. It is about understanding what works best for us and taking the time to do it.

Making self-care a priority is an important part of living an authentic life. It is about recognizing our own needs and taking the necessary steps to meet them. It is about creating a balance between our physical, mental, and emotional needs. It is also about understanding our own unique needs and taking the time to meet them. By making self-care a priority, we are investing in our own wellbeing and creating a life that is true to ourselves.

"The greatest glory in living lies not in never falling, but in rising every time we fall."

- Nelson Mandela

♡♡♡

FOURTEEN

Finding Balance in All Areas of Life

Finding balance in all areas of life is essential for living an authentic life. It can be difficult to achieve, but with the right strategies, it is possible to create harmony between your physical, mental, and emotional health.

Physical balance is achieved by taking care of your body. Eating a balanced diet, exercising regularly, and getting enough sleep are all important components of physical health. Additionally, it is important to take time for yourself to relax and unwind. This could include activities such as yoga, meditation, or simply taking a walk in nature.

Mental balance is achieved by engaging in activities that stimulate your mind. Reading, writing, and learning new skills are all great ways to keep your mind sharp. Additionally, it is important to take time to reflect on your thoughts and feelings. This could include journaling, talking to a friend, or engaging in therapy.

Emotional balance is achieved by understanding and managing your emotions. This could include recognizing when you are feeling overwhelmed and taking steps to reduce stress. Additionally, it is important to practice self-compassion and to be mindful of your thoughts and feelings.

Finding balance in all areas of life is a journey that requires dedication and commitment. It is important to be patient with yourself and to recognize that it is a process. With the right strategies, you can create harmony between your physical, mental, and emotional health and live an authentic life.

"The best way to predict your future is to create it."

- Abraham Lincoln

FIFTEEN

LIVING A LIFE OF GRATITUDE AND JOY

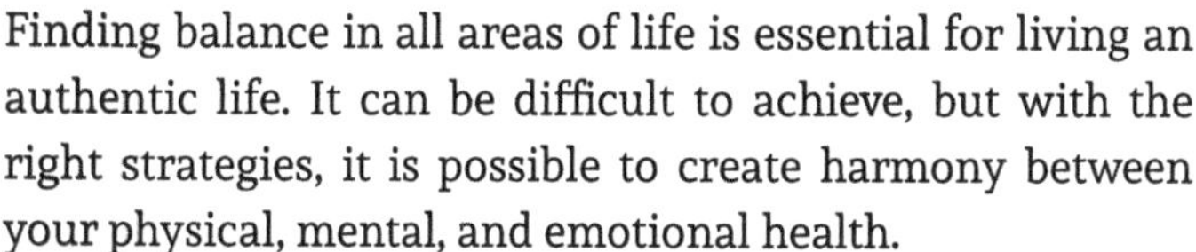

Finding balance in all areas of life is essential for living an authentic life. It can be difficult to achieve, but with the right strategies, it is possible to create harmony between your physical, mental, and emotional health.

Physical balance is achieved by taking care of your body. Eating a balanced diet, exercising regularly, and getting enough sleep are all important components of physical health. Additionally, it is important to take time for yourself to relax and unwind. This could include activities such as yoga, meditation, or simply taking a walk in nature.

Mental balance is achieved by engaging in activities that stimulate your mind. Reading, writing, and learning new skills are all great ways to keep your mind sharp. Additionally, it is important to take time to reflect on your thoughts and feelings. This could include journaling, talking to a friend, or engaging in therapy.

Emotional balance is achieved by understanding and managing your emotions. This could include recognizing when you are feeling overwhelmed and taking steps to reduce stress. Additionally, it is important to practice self-compassion and to be mindful of your thoughts and feelings.

Finding balance in all areas of life is a journey that requires dedication and commitment. It is important to be patient with yourself and to recognize that it is a process. With the right strategies, you can create harmony between your physical, mental, and emotional health and live an authentic life.

"When one door of happiness closes, another opens, but often we look so long at the closed door that we do not see the one that has been opened for us."

- Helen Keller

♡♡♡

Other Books Of The Author

1. The Moments When I Met God
2. Kashiyile Theertha Pathangal
3. GURU GYAN VANI
4. Abhiprerak Gita
5. ASSI SE JAIN GHAT TAK
6. Hopelessness of Arjuna
7. The Soul and It's True Nature
8. Sense of Action (Karma)
9. Action through Wisdom
10. Action through Wisdom
11. THEORY AND PRACTICAL OF EVERY ACTION
12. LOGICAL UNDERSTANDING OF THE SUPREME
13. THE IMPERISHABLE SUPREME
14. Yatra Nishadraj se Hanuman Ghat Tak
15. Yatra Karnatak Ghat se Raja Ghat Tak
16. Yatra Pandey Ghat se Prayagraj Ghat Tak
17. Yatra Ranjendra Prasad Ghat se Dattatreya Ghat Tak
18. YaatraSindhiya Ghat se Gwaliar Ghat Tak
19. Yatra Mangala Gauri Ghat se Hanuman Gadhi Ghat Tak
20. Yatra Gaay Ghat Se Nishad Ghat Tak
21. MAA GANGA, GHATEN EVM UTSAV
22. Ganga Arti Dev Deepavali evam Any Utsav
23. Potentials of Digitalized India
24. VEDIC CONSCIOUSNESS
25. A Brief Introduction to Vedic Science
26. Kashi ke Barah Jyotirling
27. IMPACT OF MOTIVATION
28. Let's have a Milky Way Journey
29. Color Therapy in a Nutshell

30. Rigveda in a Nutshell
31. Yajurveda in a Nutshell
32. Samveda in a Nutshell
33. Atharva Veda in a Nutshell
34. Ayushman Bhava - Ayurveda
35. Srimad Bhagavad Gita and Upanishad Connection
36. Srimad Bhagavad Gita - an attempt to summarize each chapter.
37. Facts and Impact of Nakshatra
38. Astro Gems - NAVARATNA
39. Ekadashi - A Concise Overview
40. A Concise View of Hanuman Chalisa
41. Inspirational Gita
42. Nakshatraranyam
43. Summary of 18 Mahapuranas
44. Synopsis of 18 Upa Puranas
45. Rigvediya Upanishads
46. Shukla Yajurvediya Upanishads
47. Krishna Yajurvediya Upanishads
48. Samavediya Upanishads
49. Atharvavediya Upanishads
50. The Seven Great Sages
51. From Rocket Scientist to President Dr. APJ Abdul Kalam
52. The Visionary's Voice - Quotes of Dr. APJ Abdul Kalam
53. The Wisdom of Swami Vivekananda: Insights and Inspiration from a Legendary Spiritual Teacher
54. Ayurvedic Remedies from the Garden
55. Sages and Seers
56. Rising Strong – Motivational Stories of Women
57. Beyond Flames -Mystery stories of Funeral Ghat Manikarnika
58. The Origins of Tulsi: A Look at the Mythological Roots of the Plant"

59. The Holistic Cow: A Look at the Physical, Spiritual, and Cultural Importance of Cows in India
60. Arts of Healing
61. Exploring the Divine
62. Understanding Five Elements
63. The Etymology of Ram
64. Symbols of India
65. Voice of Change (About Speeches of Great Men)
66. She Speaks (About Speeches of Great Women)
67. Patriotism on Celluloid – Brief About Patriotic Films
68. The Music of Motivation: A Brief Guide to Inspirational Film Songs
69. **Unlocking the Secrets of the Dashopanishads**
70. A Cultural Mosaic
71. Ancient Traditions, Modern Minds
72. Ecos of Ancient Wisdom
73. Beneath the Surface
74. From Temples to Ashrams
75. Sages of the Subcontinent
76. The Art of Healling (Ayurveda, Yoga & Naturopathy)
77. Indian Kitchen
78. The Festivals of India
79. The Indian Epics Retold
80. The Power of Mantras
81. The Indian River Ganges
82. The Indian Architecture
83. Rites of Passage
84. The Indian Silk Road
85. The Indian Literature
86. The Indian Villages
87. The Indian Folks & Crafts
88. The Way of Buddha
89. The Ramayan of Tulsidas

90. Astrological Remedies
91. The Secret Power of Motivation
92. Secret of Developing your Inner Strength
93. The Secret Path to Motivation
94. The Art and Secret of Positive Thinking
95. The Secrets of Practicing Ethical Living
96. Indian Art and Painting
97. The Indian Herbalism
98. Bharatanatyam to Kathak
99. Exploring India's Astrological Remedies
100. The Indian Festival of Flowers
101. Indian Handicrafts
102. The Splashes of Joy – India's Colour Festival
103. The Indian Science of Astrology
104. The Indian Mythology
105. Path to Enlightenment
106. The Indian Spirituality for Children
107. Aromas of India
108. The Secrets of Healthy Relationships
109. Ancestral Ties
110. The Indian Street Food
111. Discovering America
112. The Indian Textile
113. Listening to Motivational Speeches
114. Taste of India
115. A Cultural Journey through Indian Nuptials
116. Motivational Quote for Change
117. Secret Strategies for Making Money
118. Secrets to Cultivate a Positive Mindset
119. A Tapestry of Cultures: Exploring India from Kashmir to Kanyakumari
120. Achieving Your Dreams with Resilience: Secret Strategies for Overcoming Obstacles

121. Innovative Startups - 25 Startup Ideas to Spark Your Business Creativity
122. Export Management: Strategies for Global Success
123. Exporting from India - A Step by Step Guide
124. Finance Fundamentals: Mastering Financial Management for Business Success
125. Global Growth Strategies for International Business Development
126. Marketing Mastery: Unlocking the Secrets of Modern Marketing
127. Operations Mastery: Managing the Flow of Value in Business
128. Strategic Business Management: Navigating the Modern Business Landscape
129. Human Resource Management Strategies for Building and Managing a High Performance Team
130. The Indian Landscapes and Nature: An Exploration Of India's Natural Beauty And Diversity
131. The Indian Street Performances: A Cultural Exploration of India's Street Performances
132. Affirming Your Self-Worth: Strategies for Achieving Emotional Wellbeing
133. Cultivating Self-Discipline: Secrets Methods for Achieving Your Goals
134. Embracing Change: Strategies for Adapting to Life's Challenges
135. Embracing Your Uniqueness: Secret Strategies for Living an Authentic Life
136. Finding Motivation in Despondency: Coping with Difficult Times

Contact

DR. JAGADEESH PILLAI

MBA & PhD in Vedic Science

Four Times Guinness World Record Holder

Winner of Mahatma Gandhi Vishwa Shanti Puraskar and Global Peace Ambassador

Gemology, Astro & Vastu Consultant - Spiritual Counselor

Consultant for designing World Record Ideas

Efficient Tarot Card Reader

9839093003

myrichindia@gmail.com

drjagadeeshpillai@facebook

drjagadeeshpillai@instagram
jagadeeshpillai@youtube

www. JAGADEESHPILLAI.com

|| LOKAHA SAMASTHAHA SUKHINO BHAVANTU ||

Printed by Libri Plureos GmbH in Hamburg,
Germany